Max's Super-Special Ice Cream Invention

Story by Michael Pryor

Illustrations by Marcela Chermont

Max's Super-Special Ice Cream Invention

Text: Michael Pryor
Publishers: Tania Mazzeo and Eliza Webb
Series consultant: Amanda Sutera
  Hands on Heads Consulting
Editor: Jarrah Moore
Project editor: Annabel Smith
Designer: Jess Kelly
Project designer: Danielle Maccarone
Illustrations: Marcela Chermont
Production controller: Renee Tome

NovaStar

ISBN 978 0 17 033389 4

Cengage Learning Australia
Level 5, 80 Dorcas Street
Southbank VIC 3006 Australia
Phone: 1300 790 853
Email: aust.nelsonprimary@cengage.com

For learning solutions, visit **cengage.com.au**

Printed in China by 1010 Printing International Ltd
1 2 3 4 5 6 7 28 27 26 25 24

*Nelson acknowledges the Traditional Owners and Custodians
of the lands of all First Nations Peoples. We pay respect
to Elders past and present, and extend that respect to
all First Nations Peoples today.*

Contents

Chapter 1

The Super Top Ice Cream Shop

Every Saturday, Max and his dog, Chips, walked to the famous Super Top Ice Cream Shop at the end of his street. It was Max's favourite shop.

The owner's name was Polly Berry. She knew Max very well because he was there so often.

"Hello, Max," Polly said. She pointed at a colourful poster on the wall. "You like ice cream, so why don't you enter our competition?"

"What do I have to do?" Max asked.

"You have to invent a delicious new
ice cream flavour," Polly replied.
"If yours is the best, you will win
a free ice cream every week for a year."

Max stared. "Every week? For a whole
year?"

Polly nodded. "Any flavour you want."

Max couldn't think of anything better. "I'm going to win that competition!" he said.

Max was so excited, he ordered his favourite cherry, coconut and caramel cone.

Chips barked and ran around in a circle. He seemed excited, too, but Max wasn't going to invent a dog-food-flavoured ice cream. He was going to invent the most delicious new flavour!

Chapter 2

Two Flavours?

The next day, Max's dad helped him set up their ice cream maker. Max would just need to put in some milk and sugar, plus his special ingredients. Then he would turn on the ice cream maker to mix everything together.

Max searched the pantry. His ice cream flavour had to be something very special to win. What about coffee? No, the Super Top Ice Cream Shop already had coffee ice cream. He looked around the kitchen. Blueberry? He shook his head. Mango? No. They'd both been done before, too.

Max scratched his head. What about cheese-flavoured ice cream?
He shook his head again. Too strange.
The same for sausage ice cream, lettuce ice cream and leftover-curry ice cream.

Max picked up a jar of raspberry jam and a packet of nuts. He grinned. *Why have one flavour when you can have two?* he thought. After all, wasn't choc-mint one of the best ice cream flavours of all time? A two-flavour mix was the way to win!

Max tried mixing all sorts of ingredients, but it was no good. Everything he tried tasted awful. Tuna and canned peaches ice cream was bad. Brown sugar and onion ice cream was dreadful. Soy sauce and banana ice cream was nasty. Spaghetti and custard ice cream was horrible. Pumpkin and broken pieces of biscuit ice cream was terrible. Not even Chips was interested in *that* one.

Max sat at the bench and had some
vanilla ice cream to cheer himself up.
He had tried lots of different ingredients.
Bacon. Chilli. Tuna. Peanut butter.
Pickled onion. Ginger. Parsley. Pepper.
Nothing had worked. Nothing had tasted
delicious. He was never going to invent
a super-special ice cream flavour!

Chapter 3

Max's Big Idea

Suddenly, Max had a big idea. Two flavours together weren't working. But maybe three flavours would – just like the cherry, coconut and caramel cone he'd had at the Super Top Ice Cream Shop.

Max rubbed his chin. But for something *really* different, why stop at three ingredients? If three was good, four ingredients would be even better! How about five? Six? Even ten!

Max felt dizzy as he imagined how many ingredients he could mix together to make an amazing new ice cream flavour.

Max became very busy as he carefully added ingredients together. It took him hours as he weighed, measured, mixed and tasted. He was nearly done, and his brand-new ice cream invention was almost perfect, but it still needed a final touch.

Suddenly, Chips barked.

"That's it!" Max said. "Thanks, Chips!" He reached for the chocolate chips to complete his ice cream feast.

Chapter 4

The Winner for Sure

When the competition judging day came,
a crowd gathered at the Super Top
Ice Cream Shop. Long tables were set
up out the front. Six other children had
their new ice cream flavours in bowls.
Max joined them with the result of all his
hard work, his amazing new ice cream
invention.

Max watched carefully as Polly tried
each ice cream. She was startled by the
Porridge Ice Cream. She frowned at the
Ginger and Eggs. She scrunched up her
face at the Salty Pineapple. She shook her
head at the Pepperoni Pizza flavour.
She shuddered when she tasted the
Chilli Liquorice. She couldn't even
swallow the Garlic Strawberry.

Then Polly came up to Max.
He was nervous, but she patted him
on the shoulder. When she tasted his
Peanut Butter Bacon Pickled Onion
Coloured Sprinkles Choc Chip
Ice Cream, she took another scoop.
Then another. Then she smiled.
"This is the winner for sure!" she said.

Everyone clapped.

Max had won a free ice cream
every week for a whole year!

The next week, Max and Chips went
back to the Super Top Ice Cream Shop,
where Polly gave Max his first free cone.
Then she brought out a surprise –
a tub of special dog-food flavoured
ice cream, just for Chips!